Arthur Clark Kennedy

Erotica

Arthur Clark Kennedy

Erotica

ISBN/EAN: 9783744770972

Printed in Europe, USA, Canada, Australia, Japan

Cover: Foto ©ninafisch / pixelio.de

More available books at **www.hansebooks.com**

Erotica.

Erotica

BY

ARTHUR CLARK KENNEDY

GAY AND BIRD
LONDON
1894

TO

Contents

Life's Beauty

ALL life's beauty lies in love,
Love whose touch transposes
Barren field to flowery mead
Where the amorini tread
Ankle-deep in roses.

Let thy glamour, mighty Love,
All my youth prolong,
Youth that cannot be withstood,
Making this my solitude
Clamorous with song.

A Portrait

SHOT **gold** and shadow brown, her glorious hair
Seemeth to hold faint sunbeams tangled **where**
Its mazy ringlets cluster **o'er a brow**
Built low and broad, **which shines as** white **as snow.**
Rose-tinted cheek, straight nose, and pouting mouth,
Breath laden with all spices of the south,
Whose lips' red luscious ripeness draw my soul
Out of my breast.   Her form's distracting whole
Perfection from the tiny close-set ear
O'er shapely neck and bosom **which appear**
Smooth swelling fields to court an amorous kiss
(Ah, what a banquet for my soul were this),
Melting in gracious lines t'wards hands and **feet**
Fashioned Titania-like for any faery meet—
No fault; **no** flaw; Love spreads a cloudless sky
In her unfathomable eyes, till I,
Bending my lips to hers, become, alas, aware
That in her chin deceit lurks dimpled there.

Lord of All

To love and be **beloved,**
To snatch ripe kisses from red lips of youth
Is of a truth
Earth's utmost blessing, this **even I** have proved.

To kiss and clasp fresh charms
In eager arms,
To wring Love's moisture from the inmost core
Of a deep heart and hunger still for more,
Is to be lord of Love.

Sweetheart, when thou and I,
In very ecstasy,
Transfuse our souls in death,
Each panting amorous breath
But wafts us to the sky.

The goal of our desire
We reach with brain on fire,
But reach it to expire.

Alas, how low the fall
When passions duller burn;
Then Life begins to spurn
Love that will not return;
And Death is lord of all.

A Vision

Lo, all her body clothed with love,
Meet for the kisses of a King,
My lady cometh, and the spring
Scatters its sweetness from above.

Through gates of horn she issueth,
Down pathways of the land of dreams,
Her footsteps softly **fall, she seems**
Re-risen from the hand of **death.**

The violets bud beneath her tread,
The teeming earth in tongues of flame
Spits lambent crocus shoots, with shame
Each challenged snowdrop hangs its **head.**

She stands and stretches out to me
Her white arms, whiter than desire,
Some seven times heated in God's fire;
All Love's alluring bravery

Glows in her slight transfigured frame,
My heart throbs wildly in my breast,
Charged with vague yearnings, long supprest
As her lips move to form my **name.**

But ere one syllable can **pass**
Those **red lips where** my lips **have** kissed,
The vision rolls up like a mist,
Or breath that fadeth from a glass,

Leaving me lone with longing cries
Choked backward, whilst my surcharged sight
Aches sparklingly, as closing night
Thickens its pressure on my eyes.

Take Thou My Love

TAKE thou my love, I give it all to thee
As space far-reaching, deep **as the deep sea,**
It grew for thee alone, and only thee,
　　Take thou my love.

Heed not the love that others offer thee,
Dregs of some other love's satiety,
Mere bankrupts are they, spending thriftlessly;
　　Heed **not** their **love.**

Take, then, my love, 'tis Fate's ordained decree,
Let it encompass, thrill through, melt in thee,
Making us one to all eternity;
　　Take, then, my love.

Regeneration

Lo ! Love leaned o'er thy cradle at thy birth,
And laid his lips on thine a moment's space,
Breathing faint laughter and desire of mirth
Into thy soul, and something not of earth
Now mocks me from thy face.

Fain would I raise an answer in those eyes
My hungry eyes look into, but there lurks
Low laughter in their depths, like radiant skies
That from their azure battlements despise
Earth's earnest toilsome works.

8

They float above the knowledge of things gross,
Serenely still and smiling through the void,
And yet methinks theirs is an unknown loss,
Not theirs contrasted peace, nor tempests' toss
Followed by calms enjoyed.

So will I pray that Love's lips set their seal
Once more on thine, that thou be born again
Of this earth earthy; let Love's lips reveal
Secrets of laughter turned to tears and deal
Out Love's delicious pain.

Love's Guidance

GIVE me thy hand and guide me, Love,
Where golden blossoms gem those fields
Through which Life's waters gently move
Bearing the lilies' silver shields
Upon her breast, past lowing herds,
Neath shady haunts of building birds
Whose carols greet the Spring when yields
Nature to Love.

When Spring is past stay with me, Love,
When wolds lie panting under June,
When tempering earthward tears to prove
Heaven's pity cease to fall, we swoon
Wrapped in heat's hazy hanging mist
With seeming far-off souls and list
To that immeasurable tune
Nature plays Love.

When whiter weather holds the land
In iron chains and shrill alarms
The north winds blow, take thou my hand
Again, Oh Love, and from all harms
Bred errant ways withdraw my feet,
Leading me to thy kingdom sweet,
Of changeless skies, where in thine arms
Enfold me, Love!

Above Sonnenburg

THE crumbling ruins of the past
Are left behind and on the hill
We rest our horses and **are** still;
Thought alone stirs, while **from** the vast
Stone quarries sounds the clinking drill.

So, loved one, leave behind **the** strife
And wreckage of your past; we'll **take**
Fresh stone from the fair future, make
Ourselves a house of light **and** life;
Your eyes **were** sealed, you now awake.

12

The Sleeping Beauty

SHE slept whilst chains of servitude
Were round her rivetted,
Her palace walls were hung about
With cere-cloths of the dead,
The rank weeds sprang within her courts,
Wild briars fenced her gate ;
For seven long years the spell had worked—
Comes then the Prince too late?

Lo ! from her fair limbs fall the chains,
The rank weeds fade away ;
Her Prince awakes her with a kiss
And knowledge brings the day.

13

Spring

Unchain your heart, cast off the bands
Imposed by social customs' care,
By laws of man. Be free as air—
Shake off those so-called friendly hands

That hold **you** back from following
The dictates Nature planted there,
List to her voice within your ear!
"**Awake and** love, **it** is the Spring."

My Love, awake. It is the Spring!
Let all the envious world roll by,
Above us bends the bright blue sky
Where mounts the lark on fluttering wing

The distant cooing of the dove,
The blackbird, linnet, **finch** and thrush,
In madrigals from every bush
And varied accents, **say** " We love."

'Tis good to live, 'tis good to love—
God's greatest gift, so freely given,
To man below, foretaste of heaven
Has come to us, let us then prove

Its golden value **in the scales**
'Gainst earthly gold. The merest **dross**
And tinsel seems earth's gold. **The loss**
Of all the world holds dear avails

Nothing against such perfect wealth
As **we** in Love's own land to-day
Gather with both hands. Let us pray
That Love walk hand in hand with Health.

Health is for Love a fitting mate,
And on such guardian's rainbow wings
We well may pass Earth's fiery rings
And smile contempt on sordid Fate.

Carpe Diem

LET us learn all that love can teach,
Dear heart, while we and love are young;
Too soon, alas, Life's bark will reach
Those sandy shores, that thirsty beach,
Lashed by the sad wave's tongue.

For Love will land us on that strand
Strewn with gaunt ribs of former wrecks,
If we, indifferent to command,
Handle no ropes, but idly stand
Along the uncared-for decks.

Star Worship

WHOSO adores a star
Must worship it afar,

Until one day, mayhap,
'Twill drop into his lap.

And then, for such are men,
He'll cast it forth again.

He only loves a star
Who worships it afar.

I Love My Love

I LOVE my Love because my Love loves me.
Ah! that she did so as I'd fain be loved
With love by which the mountains may be moved,
Uprooted and cast in the midmost sea.

Such love surpassing, deep and broad and high,
O'ershadowing all things else in earth, in heaven,
Love unalloyed at morn, at noon, at even,
Love unalloyed when darkness holds the sky.

A Love that overcometh and will prove
Itself through storm and sunshine, frost and fire;
A Love which naught can change, which naught
    can tire,
Even Death's self can not destroy such love.

So, Sweet, let me set seal upon your mouth
And lie within your arms' encircling fold,
Gaze in your eyes, and in their depth behold
Twin starry loves **whilst** all the balmy South

Gives up her richest spices in your breath,
When heart tumultuously doth beat on heart,
The while our spirits mingle ne'er to part
Wholly again, though earthly ties by Death

Are severed, 'tis but for a time, and then
Our spirits will commingle and commune,
Each with the other strung to Love's one tune
And the sweet memories of what has been.

For past and present still to us belong,
To you and I, dear Love, then wherefore waste
Thoughts on the unknown future, rather taste
The sweets of life and do not call it wrong

To be too happy. Let us therefore cast
An offering to the Gods like those of eld
Strove to appease the Deity who held
The compensating balances. **And last,**

When this life's cup is drunken to the lees,
Leaving its after-taste upon your tongue,
You yet will kiss my lips with lips unwrung
By bitterness regretful. On my knees

I pray you, Sweetheart, to be wise in time.
You cannot change the Ethiop's dusky skin!
The leopard's spots! So leave him with his sin
Ere his contagion drags you through more slime.

The false God whom you worshipp'd shall lie dead,
His groves hewn down, his altar overthrown;
Peace, happiness, and love shall be your own,
Three golden halos hung above your head.

For you have eaten of the tree of life
After the tree of knowledge, and shall live
Another life, and all the past shall give
Its blackness up, its sorrow, sin, and strife,

To form a background for the fair "to be,"
Which we'll embroider with love's golden skein
The story of your past, of false love slain
And true love shrined upon its memory.

The past shall be a dream; you will awake
And wonder could such things have ever been.
Your scars of slavery which now are green
Shall **be** no more. You will arise and take

Within your grasp that fellow hand which Fate
At length has guided to its destined end.
We grope the whole world round until we bend
Our steps predoom'd through Love's celestial gate.

Even though I were Dead

EVEN though I were dead,
Cold, and divorced from men,
My heart would leap up again
In hurried throbs at **your tread,**
Passing it overhead.

Had We but Met

AH, Love, had we but met before,
When standing at the gate of life,
Ere we had opened wide that door—
Now, I a husband, you a wife,
Have met too late. Ah, say not so,
You would have loved me years ago.

Then **why** not now! What earthly ties
Made by mankind can bind our souls
Which rush together! Let us rise
Above such bondage. What controls
A love like ours? 'Tis not of earth,
But from Promethean fires has birth.

22

'Tis no low-born **material** flame,
Fanned by the breath **of** lustful **men,**
That flickers fiercely first, then tame,
Then fiercely once again, and then
Dies down into grey embers, cold
Because this life seems growing **old !**

Nay, let our love, Sweet, vanquish **Time,**
Cast out all fear, forget the past
And its attendant ills—sublime
Stretches the future's vista—vast
Potentialities therein,
To love **is surely** not **a sin !**

'Tis **far** more sinful, Sweet, to **me,**
To yield yourself up to abuse
Of lust in guise of love, than be
Freely beloved. That man's vile use,
Though sanctioned by our social creed,
Has left your body poor indeed.

Question and Answer

SHE

WHEN Time has robbed me of my years,
And tell-tale lines invest my eyes
With channels ploughed by dint of tears,
Whilst here and there a hair appears
Turned **silver by** Time's sighs.

For he has come quite unawares
And breathed his sighs upon my head,
Whilst **I,** weighed down with earthly cares
Have recked not of the passing years,
But sought my daily bread.

24

Love, will you love me as you say
You love me now, when I am old
And all my beauty fades away,
Like autumn tints when turning gray
Leave life a tale near told.

HE

I love you not for what you **were**
Or what you are, though silver **gleams**
May nestle in your sunny **hair,**
And envious crows plant feet of care
About your eyes, my hourly dreams

Hold but your image, sweetest heart,
Deep set within a shrine of gold,
With it I live a life apart
Where time is not, and like my art,
You never can grow old.

Once

SHE kissed me once, 'twas long ago,
But something subtle in me stirred
As if the vans of some great bird
Had fanned my blood into a glow
'Twas something wasteful, wild yet sweet,
Intangible, without a name,
But through my veins with sudden heat
It passed and burst into a flame—
'Twas molten once that lava stream,
Ran with red riotings, but now

26

It cannot melt the winter snow
That time has piled upon my brow!
Oh! Time, how long ago it seems
Since first I dreamt those golden dreams
And in Love's school remained a dunce.
You've robbed my locks of pristine sheen,
But there's one memory always green,
Immutable, you cannot steal ;
For still, 'twixt dusk and dawn I feel
The kiss with which she kissed me once.

'Twixt Ivory Pales

RONDEAU

'TWIXT ivory pales uprose a precious dome,
A shrine thatched over where no man might come,
For vestals only could the entrance win
To worship her who sat enthroned therein—
A Goddess fresh begotten of the foam.

Until one day I that way chanced to roam,
Half open stood the gateway in the gloom,
Revealing splendours of the shrine within
'Twixt ivory pales.

28

Marshalling my forces without beat of drum,
The next dark night when Nature' face was dumb,
I forced the ward and swiftly entered in
Regardless of the sacrilege and sin.
The shrine was mine—and now I call it home
         'Twixt ivory pales.

How Shall I Woo Thee?

How shall I woo thee, Love?
Under the lang'rous noon,
Bringing thee roses red
And redder gold, to spread
Speech till thy senses swoon?
Or when the twilight falls,
With the soft aid
Of music, heavenly maid,
Scaling thy walls?

How shall I **win** thee, Love?
Standing forth **in the** sun,
Claiming thee **as** the meed
Of some heroic deed
Greatly dared, greatly done?
Or with my wistful eyes,
Flattering thy sunny face,
Praising thy stately grace,
Silence's **prize**?

How shall I wear thee, **Love?**
Throned mid the **flaunted crowd,**
Lifted aloft and **crowned**
With men's applause, **the sound**
Making me proud?
Or shrined within my heart,
Hidden where none may come,
Under a golden dome
Always apart.

Possession

Around my neck her soft arms twine,
My kisses fleck her bosom's snow,
Her breath intoxicates like wine,
And sends the blood's imperious flow
Mantling across my eyes; I know
At last that she is wholly mine.

And I am hers. Each pulse of me
Beats red rebellion, and each vein
Swells with an overwhelming sea
Of sad, glad, pleasurable pain
Pervading every sense, my brain
Throbs with a mad intensity.

32

Passing through realms of star and cloud,
Scaling the mountains of the moon,
My soul ascends, my body bowed
O'er her fair form in seeming swoon,
Unstrung by Love's almighty tune,
Reels far below; sensations crowd

Upon sensations, like the waves
Follow waves shorewards, so they beat
Upon my being; each one paves
The way for its successor's feet
To follow faster, till with heat
Made faint, they trip among the graves

Of former joys; confused they fall
Dead 'mid dead ashes scattered there.
Earthbound once more, and stripped of all
Illusions, through the breathless air
My soul sinks slowly back, aware
Of waiting Sleep's incorporate pall.

In Italy

GIVE us the sun and give us love,
A western breeze on a sapphire sea,
Heaven below and heaven above,
Heaven for thee and me.

A western breeze to fan our sails
Lazily flapping against the mast,
Facing the ocean with rippling scales
Drawing to port at last,

As we hail our casa's whited walls,
Where olive-trees gemm'd with the fireflies' light
Stand fringing the groves whence Philomel calls
To the liquid soul of night.

34

And scents lie heavy upon **the air,**
From orange blossoms cloying **the breath,**
And a soothing hum that **numbs the ear**
Comes from the town beneath.

Till a mist creeps over the hill, shuts down
On our home's white walls and o'erhanging **eaves,**
And the nightingales hush as the distant town
Puts out her lights and **leaves**

The rest of the night to darkness **and love**
Consecrated to thee and me,
Whilst my world spins on about and above,
Centred in thee.

Changes

THE sea is the same, yet not the same,
The sky is the same, yet not the sky
That was over our heads when we hitherward came
Just a year ago, **my** Love **and I.**

For then, my Love, you loved me **true,**
Blue was the sea **and** blue the **sky,**
Beautiful both in their azure hue,
But colours will fade and love will die.

Cold and grey are **the sea** and sky,
Waves **are** swelling against the shore,
Bearing **you** far from me ; and I
List to their crooning of 'nevermore.'

An Appeal

My love is all too great for **speech,**
The words that swell upon my **tongue**
Fall still-born back, unsaid, **unsung ;**
    Canst not divine
The mute appeal that shines from each
Of my soul's windows, lit within
By burning love, yet does not win
    Return from thine ?

O, let one answering look appease
The thirst of life's parched desert lands,
Down the long reaches of whose sands
    I wander lone,
Then shall the wilderness with trees
Bud, in whose branches all day long
Birds shall awake and break in song
    For thee mine own.

Love the Voyager

YOUNG Love unfurled his silken sail,
And in his boat **of** ivory pale
Went sliding down the **weather.**
By sunny shores of golden isles
Their hills o'ertopped for miles on miles
With ruddy helms **of** heather.

Over seas to a shady bay,
Where, lotus-locked, enchanted lay
He and his boat together,
Unwotting of the days that flew
In one long monotone of blue,
From waning summer's tether.

39

Till heaven darkened, and the rain,
Smoking athwart the watery plain,
Fell down with wintry weather;
Then, like **a lark** that upward flies,
Love swiftly lessened through the skies,
On winnowing **feather.**

But the poor boat drifts on, resigned
To furies of the wave and wind,
And wintry weather.

A Reflection

HOLDING a mirror in an idle hand,
I chanced to breath thereon,
When through the film there gleamed
A sudden face that seemed
Hers I had made my own
Once in that far-off sunny stranger land,

Once, and once only, had I **held** her, kissed
Her eyes that through her hair
Shone starlike, lit with heat
From fires that throbbed and beat
In her brown bosom bare,
Long blanch'd since then beneath Time's nether mist.

I had not thought of her for years on years,
Nor thought I of her when
I breathed, and brought her back
Down memory's vagrant track,
Sweet even now as then,
But seen, alas, through blurring haze of tears

That sprang unbidden to my startled eyes,
When that face on my gaze
Burned sudden-wise, and I
Bent down with a great cry,
As in those far-off days
I bent to her red mouth 'neath alien skies.

Though the film fading from the surface glass
Banished her from my mind,
It left a sharp regret
That rankles even yet
Implanted there behind,
For that lost day, regret that will not pass.

Oh Love, my Love, I love you so

LIKE petals shaken from a rose
Beneath the noontide heat,
So fell her loving words on him
Where he knelt at her feet,
In tender accents, sweet and low,
"Oh Love, my Love, I love you so !

"I love you, love me, or I die,
Fainting beneath Love's fire
Which burns my very life-blood black
By breath of my desire.
Kiss these my bosoms white as snow,
And quench their flame's devouring glow.

43

"Freely I yield myself to you,
Throne you my King, my Lord,
Your smile a crown of light to me,
Your frown a very sword.
Oh Love, my Love, I love you so,
Your silence strikes me as a blow."

Then he replied with heart too full
For any sudden speech,
By holding up his arms to her,
And as each clung to each,
Mixed with the fountain's murmurous flow
I heard "Oh Love, I love you so!"

That long kiss sanctified a year,
A month, a week, a day.
Perhaps 'twas but an hour, who knows?
Time stays for such as they.
Love counts not time, but this I know,
'Twas very, very long ago.

She Walked Through Fire

Pure, untouched, even as she came
She passed, unsullied and the same,

SHE walked through fire, a hungry flame
Leapt up to lick and lap her o'er,
Then backward flung its head in shame,
Nor crisped the letters of her **name,**
Along the glowing ashen floor.
Spotless amid **a** motley crew
She passed the fiery ordeal through
Unhurt, begirt as with a fence
Of innocence.

45

Joyous she was, and ever gay,
Though an occasional April day
Would steal across her heaven. For her
The flames were bright and beautiful,
And each tongue seemed to minister
A pleasant warmth unto her soul ;
Her light-breathed laughter drove them back
To line the path her feet would track,
Her sunny tears reflected them.

Ah, happy, happy, wayward child,
Bright contradiction, when you smiled
Upon the flames, they danced in glee,
Or crept to kiss and clasp your knee,
As suppliants subdued and tame.

How did you pass those fiery ways,
And come from out the midmost blaze
No smell of burning on your hair ?

Because my love o'ershadowed you,
Because your heart was pure and true
Where'er you were.

Kismet

We both shed many bitter tears,
But married in the after **years,**
    And then
We once more parted. In the **street,**
As strangers now, we never greet
    Each other.
I saw you walking yesterday,
Beside you, slightly streaked with grey,
    Your brother,
Reminding **me** of years that range
Against us. Soon the latest change
    Will come,

47

O'er you, o'er me, o'er him, o'er all,
The summoning funereal
            To Home.
            And when
Absolved from this world's toil and heat,
I wonder shall we ever meet
            Again?
For in that other world the dead
Know each and all things—so 'tis said—
            And there
The words that here Pride could not say
For once and all would clear away
            Despair.

My Cot

I own a dainty little cot
Begirt about with **roses,**
Standing in **a** shady **spot**
Amid most verdant closes.

The door was bolted, locked **and barred,**
All entrance was denied there,
They vainly sought **to** force **the ward**
Who tried before **I tried there.**

They tried with gold **and** silver keys,
With vows and protestations,
They summoned every art **to** please,
Exotics of **all** nations.

Then others with a diamond tried
To cut the window pane,
But still the entrance was **denied,**
Their labour was in vain.

The house, to **whom did** it belong,
And I possession win?
I breathed myself into a song,
And so I entered in.

Francesca

STATELY she moved, **my lady,** through the **wood,**
With lingering footfalls following her own thought
Which like a child at random, heeding naught,
Sped on before, one **of a merry brood**
As yet by **Love** untaught.

Upon the turf I **lay** in musing mood,
Pillowed by some gnarl-rooted forest tree,
And watched that **vision** passing silently
As in a dream, till all at once she stood
Struck still **at** sight of me.

Twin starry sapphires swinging in her ears
Gave silent challenge to her liquid eyes
Which challenged mine awhile in mute surmise
Or e'er she spake.—Even so across **the** years
She cometh to me yet, but veiled, alas, with tears.

A Lustrum

A LUSTRUM has not sped since first we met.
How many shall have ere we meet again?
Thou hast gone forth from this our world of pain
Leaving me heavy-hearted, with eyes wet,
Before my manhood's empty shrine—and yet
I'd fain believe we did not love in vain.

"One Year Saw Twain Made One"

ONE year saw twain made one
And one become as three,
Then he remained alone
For they had ceased to be.
Fair graft and blossom failing left a scarrèd tree!

— O solitary soul,
Not here, nor yet, thy goal.

A Queen

A QUEEN—he loved her,
His queen—he moved her
For she was human.

Ermine robes, jewelled crown,
Thrust aside, **thrown down,**
Left but a woman.

And did they blame her?
Or could it shame her?
No! love became her.

Who Is She?

DEAR women pass before me in my dreams,
Dear women dead whose red lips I have kissed,
In sweet succession smiling through a mist
Of many unshed tears, but yet it seems
One woman stands behind me, who is she?

She stands behind me silently. Alas,
I cannot see, but feel her presence there,
The soft reflected radiance of her hair
Lights up the gloom, but still she will not pass,
This ever silent woman, who is she?

For hunger of this woman yet **unseen,**
Whose presence felt is seared **upon my brain,**
My heart pervaded by **her scent is fain**
To beat **no more** for **women who have** been,
Or are, but only **for her. Who is she?**

Stay, Oh Day

DAY is lying dying,
Comes the night.
Fate is flying, flying,
Take thou hold of fate,
Or at least by trying
To arrest his flight,
A short respite buying,
Still there may be light,
And too late
Comes the night.

Doth Love but live in daylight?
Love is blind.
Daylight or the dark
Love's electric spark
Makes Earth's darkness bright.
Night is day—day, night,
Equal in his sight,
Love is blind.

Still night will come at last,
And the skies
Denser shadows cast
Where Love lies,
Surfeited and weary,
While the twilight dreary
Deepens, darkens, dies.
Life and love are past
At the last.

Wert Cold and Chill

WERT cold and chill
In thy death-trance lying,
I'd pluck thee still
From the midmost dying,'
A cure for thine ill
With my heart-blood buying.

Thy cheeks' pale ashes
Should burn and glow,
Through lifting lashes
Thy soul should show
Redeemed from the cachés
Of under-woe.

E'en death's endeavour
Were vain to part,
For I'd hold thee ever
Against my heart,
Allaying its fever
And passionate smart.

Love Given and Denied

A LOVE, that one would give his soul to win
And an hereafter heaven,
Denied unto his life's devotion
Is lightly given
Unto a false emotion.
A few low words, soft hand-clasps, shaded eyes
Of passing thoughtful carelessness, the prize
Falls from its place into 'what might have been.'

Sweet Contradiction

SWEET contradiction is **the soul**
Of **every** woman. When **I burned**
With love, poured passionate words, 'heart **whole**
She laughed, but **when** aside I turned
To note another's wistful look
Whence spake a world unutterable,
At once she stood between us, took
My hand in hers, her bosom rose and fell,
Her eyes she kept downcast **a** little space,
And then her lips were lifted to my **face.**

63

Dear Little Feet

Dear little feet which fain must press
The ways of this world's wickedness,
    When older grown,
May God send down His brightest rays
To guide ye through the stir and stress,
Into the paths of prayer and praise
    Towards His throne.

64

Because

BECAUSE in **years ago**
Two people lived **and loved,**
Because two hearts **were moved**
By the same mighty throe
That thrilled them through **and through,**
A nation is **alive.**

A nation is alive,
Though he **and she are dead.**
From that glad marriage-bed
Their spirits still survive,
And to the ages give
Their immortality.

65   F

Their immortality,
Blent in their children's child,
Glad, sad or mad, or mild,
What was, still is, must be,
Like the eternal sea,
Ever in ebb and flow.

Ever in ebb and flow
Their immortality
Beats onward like the **sea.**
Because in years ago
Two people lovèd, lo !
A nation is alive.

I Called in Vain

I CALLED in vain unto the night,
To shew me heaven and heaven's God ;
I asked the sea who ruled her might
    As with a rod.

I asked of **all** the winds the same,
If they too served this unknown God,
And from his footstool went and came,
    Swayed by his nod.

I sought an answer **from** a star,
But it hung in the voiceless void,
And on my quest I wandered far
        Unsatisfied.

Until I whispered to the ground,
" O, Mother Earth, canst thou not prove
That such exist?" and then I found
My heaven, your arms ; my God, your love !

Revolution

My **bed** still bears the imprint of thy form,
A faint perfume still hangs upon the air,
Like dying roses, but no longer warm
This breast so **wont** thy loveliness to wear.

Mere outline of what was, **the** skeleton
Of former joyfulness denied me **now** ;
The shrine is empty and no **queen** upon
My heart's throne reigns **with** love-anointed brow.

The queen is dead. Set up another queen.
Nay, for their reign is over, and I can
No more support such despots. They have been.
I'll rule myself, a state republican.

69

Who Goes Home?

RONDEAU

WHEN "Who goes home?" a voice stentorian calls,
Re-echoing through corridors and halls,
  To faithful Commons **met** in grave debate,
  When lights are lowered and the hour is late,
Grateful on weary ears that summons falls.

Slowly with shadowy footsteps sleep installs
Silence within old Westminster's grey walls,
Peace reigns in place of party passionate
    When all go home.

70

When thinner blood through this my body crawls,
And slackening sense is bound in Death's dark thralls,
  Love, shall I find you waiting at the gate
  With open arms? Ah! may that be my fate
    When I go home.

FINIS.

ERRATUM.—Page 31, *for* "**flaunted**" *read* "flaunting."

Printed by R. Folkard & Son, 22, Devonshire St., Queen Sq., London.

www.ingramcontent.com/pod-product-compliance
Lightning Source LLC
Chambersburg PA
CBHW021426090426
42742CB00009B/1280